Grandpa's Birthday

by Sofia Garcia
illustrated by Terry Widener

Scott Foresman
is an imprint of

Glenview, Illinois • Boston, Massachusetts • Mesa, Arizona
Shoreview, Minnesota • Upper Saddle River, New Jersey

Illustrations
Terry Widener

Photographs
Every effort has been made to secure permission and provide appropriate credit for photographic material. The publisher deeply regrets any omission and pledges to correct errors called to its attention in subsequent editions.

Unless otherwise acknowledged, all photographs are the property of Pearson Education, Inc.

12 ©Sam Diephuis/Corbis

ISBN 13: 978-0-328-39404-3
ISBN 10:   0-328-39404-1

Jandro's family flew to Mexico for Grandpa's birthday party. Jandro talked nonstop. He had many questions about Mexico.

They reached Grandpa's house.
"Jandro, please join me on a walk,"
Grandpa said. "I insist."
"Now you can learn about Mexico!"
said Jandro's father.

Jandro walked with Grandpa.
Midway through town, they saw a
church. People were leaving a wedding.
    A bridesmaid said, "Hello, Jandro. I
am an old friend of your mother's. I'll
see you at the birthday party."

Jandro and Grandpa walked to
the market.

"Hello, Santos," shouted Grandpa
to a man peering at them. "Come and
meet my grandson, Jandro!"

"Hello, Jandro," said Santos. "Your
father came to this market when he
was a boy."

Jandro saw a pretty ring. He bought it for his mother.

"I think she would like that," said Grandpa. "Your mother shopped here with your Aunt Ana when they were young."

Jandro put the ring in his pocket so that he would not misplace it.

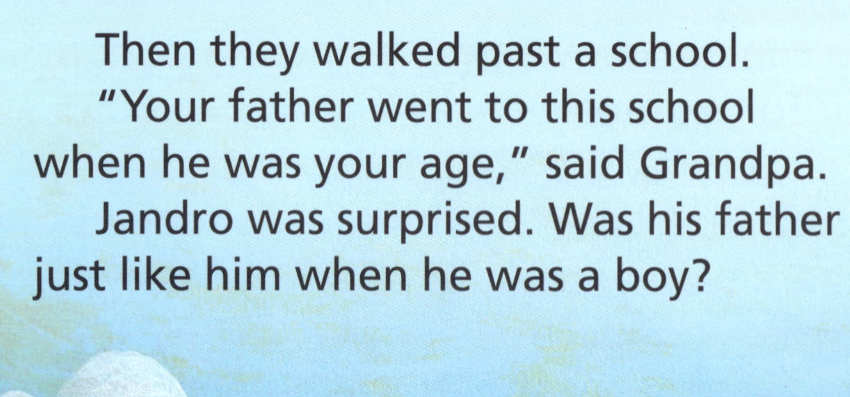

Then they walked past a school.
"Your father went to this school
when he was your age," said Grandpa.
Jandro was surprised. Was his father
just like him when he was a boy?

They returned to the house. The first guest arrived. The party had officially begun! Jandro saw the bridesmaid from the church and his Aunt Ana. Santos brought a piñata. Some of Grandpa's friends were there too.

"Did you like seeing the town?" asked Jandro's father.

"Yes," said Jandro. "I met a lot of people."

"They are all very important to our family," said his father.

Jandro liked seeing the place where his parents had once lived.

"Can we please come to Grandpa's party every year?" he begged.

Piñatas

Read Together

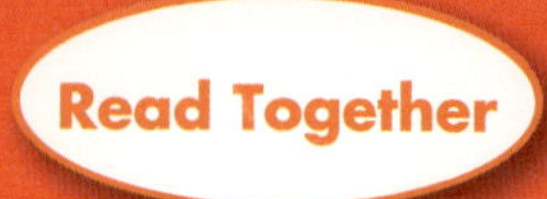

Piñatas are colorful paper shapes filled with candy, fruit, and small toys. They usually hang on a rope from a ceiling or tree branch. Children wearing blindfolds swing sticks to break the piñatas. When a piñata breaks, the things inside spill onto the ground. Children then run to collect the treats.

Children in Mexico have enjoyed playing with piñatas for a long time. Today, piñatas bring fun to holiday and birthday celebrations in countries all over the world.

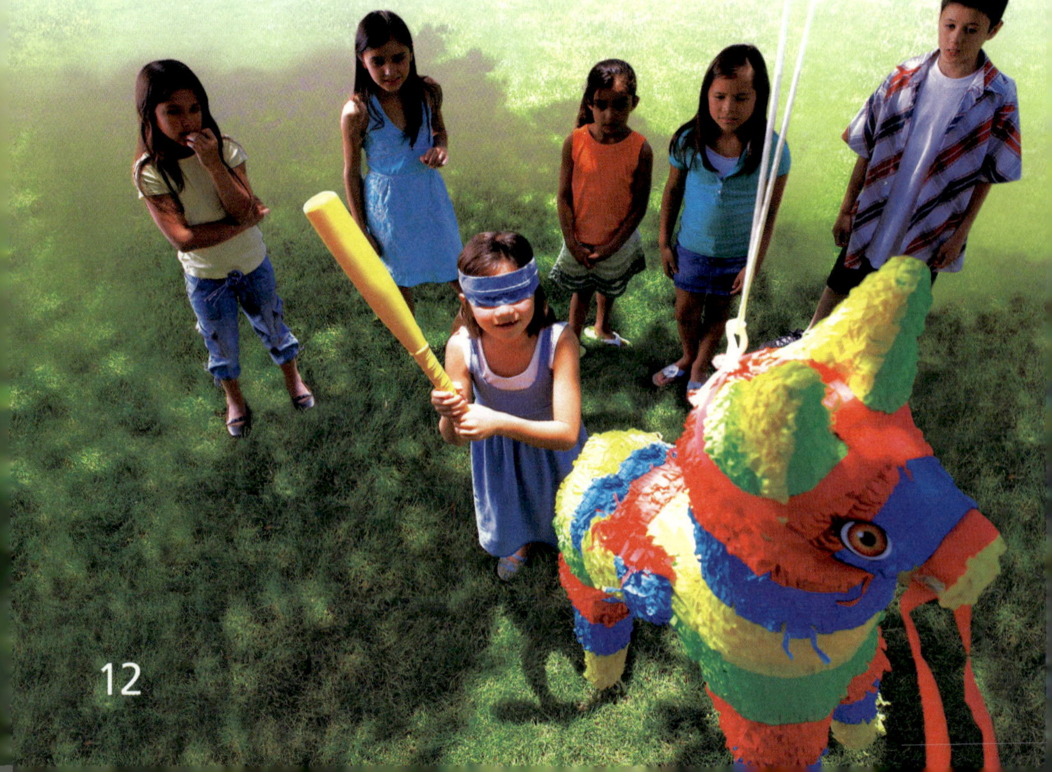